The wildflower's misadventures

Jom Laus

BookLeaf Publishing

India | USA | UK

Presentation by *BookLeaf Publishing*

Web: www.bookleafpub.com

E-mail: info@bookleafpub.com

ISBN: 9789360942588

First edition 2024

To the two women in my life, that forever lives in my heart, Mom Grace and Mama Linda.

PREFACE

"The ache for home lives in all of us." — Maya Angelou

Drive Home

weary weary eyes,
roads at three o' nine.
the only good thing at sight,
Is I'll be home by daylight.

Dystopian Paradise

2

my feet buried itself in the cool waters,
and the sunlight slipped through my fingers,
the smell of grass, and the whisper of the wind,
my lover's hand reaching for me...

my worries fade, as I bask in this paradise...

I blink slowly, and find my chest heavy.

an empty bed, my covers damp from last night's
tears
I circle around in nothingness.

for a moment I found my paradise,
for a moment I thought home was in front of my
eyes.
for a moment.

Cascade

I gather all my belongings,
eager to find what my dreams were;

The city scapes, the bustle of the streets,
a whole new person was forming.

It only needed to be a month or two,
to figure out maybe this isn't me;
and tell myself "Hey, this isn't you!"

hurt, after hurt.
confusion slowly growing.
the passing of lessons like water cascading down
a cliff.

Who am I in this journey?
Can someone tell my father, this is not where I
want to be.

Pine Tree City

Cold breezes and wind chimes,
I've had memories here,
both bittersweet and sublime.

I adore the children laughing in the street,
I enjoy the food and the fog that kisses my
cheek.

The rain makes me sullen,
the sun makes smug.
I think I found love in this city,
and also encountered bad luck.

This place feels like my second home,
a place where my heart continues to long for
a place where nothing is a bore.

City of Pines, you're a wonder to me.
Have you always been this dreamy?

Airfare

5

There are two things you shouldn't worry about splurging on:

Time and airfare.

The journey home and the journey out of home is always something to look forward to.

new found land

So I sail in the winds of despair,
but the smell of greener grass is there.

I cannot comprehend why this new found land is
where it all begins,
and why the home I knew felt like it was so hard
to fit in.

Letters

And was this the only way?
I had to leave you,
be a thousand miles away.
for you to realize,
home never felt the same?

I wrote those letters to remind you of how I
loved you,
and how you lost me, in this journey.

What was it?

8

It wasn't luck at all.
Perhaps it was hard work.
Perhaps it was those late nights I stayed up.
Perhaps it was the extra effort I gave.

Most likely, it was the sincerest prayers I have
prayed.

Whatever it was, I am where I am exactly where
I need to be.

And so the story goes..

9

a little child wrapped in her mother's arms.
a little child longing for his father's smile.

no matter where I went, I have a child in my
heart that needed to be held.

and so I protected it with the bigger, stronger,
person.
yet every time I fought, the punches got through
this little kid;

I had most of the blow, but the
bruises still showed.

How can I build a home where this inner child
could heal?

Snowfall

When the snow lands on those warm little hands
of yours,
when the happiness settles in, and when your
eyes glisten
in the sparkly sight of the ice covered land.

I hope it stays.

I hope the cold doesn't seep in, I hope it doesn't
remind you of how frost, really bites. And how
loneliness seeps in through your being.

Just like how snow is only water, in different
form.

Beautiful but dangerous.

I belong to the warmer weather.

Lost and lost

There is beauty in not knowing,
there is beauty of the unseen,
there is beauty in the longing
for what might could have been.

There is sadness in the opportunities I've missed,
there is sadness when I think I wish we could
have just kissed.

You come and sweep across my path, now I'm
lost all over again.

mango trees

12

She sat down, plotting her next move.
crooked smile and wide eyes,
"this looks like a great adventure", she mouthed.

There is a road where people take full of mango
trees and river, and lakes.
There is a road where people take that cover the
sun, trees too high and mountains so steep.

You will only row the boat of life with callused
hands and barefoot dreams,
but you can never guarantee tomorrow until you
take the first step, I'm afraid that's how it seems.

Walk with me

And so this Man has called me unto His lap,
His eyes were as deep as the ocean,
and His voice sounded like lullabies.

Although His features were gentle,
my knees trembled and I shuddered.

I felt like in my life, I walked past by Him a
thousand times.
Forgetting He was there. Ignoring He was there.

But He always came at the right moments,
always waiting.

so I Hold him tight, as he told me, "Come walk
with me, child"

And so I did, for the rest of my life.

Discoveries

So does the sky really look blue to you?
Why did the ostrich run but never fly?
Is the moon in your place higher tonight than
mine?
If stars were eyes from above, do they also cry?
Why am I missing a place, I've never been to?

a micro poem.

Brisbane

15

The night is cold,
A silence so bold.
A thousand miles away,
loneliness makes me their prey…

a micro poem.

Belmont

there are four walls in this space,
there are three words I need to stay,
there are only two people in this place,
only one goes home tonight.

a micro poem.

The 6,827 miles

There could be sparklers and wine,
there are cocktails and a fine dine.

The coins keep coming, endless shopping.
you name it, you can buy it.

although, you like this place they call the
highland,
it cannot compare to the little island.

The little island stuck on your head,
6,827 miles.

Home can never be replaced.

Yellow dresses

18

Does growing up mean we have to walk steps
that are a hundred, thousand, steps away from
home?

Does it mean, losing interest in all that made you
happy
as a child?

Why does it feel like I'm leaving the only place I
felt safe at,
for a place I know nothing about?

I twirled around my yellow dress, and the world
just spun around with it.

The 20422

I dragged my tired soul into bed that night,
my hands trembling and tears welled up.

I held unto every hope and prayer I have,
I've yearned for time with you,
I was still a little kid, longing for you.

it didn't feel like I was safe,
personally, it felt like hell.

Eyes set on water

20

So the depths of the sea I voyage,
I wait and wait for all the little ripples
to disappear...

I wait for the wind to stop.
And I travelled the bright clouds,
and I soared with the birds.

This life is meant to be explored,
so I continue to go wherever life takes me.

Home is where your heart is

21

If you are searching,
If your heart is still truly finding a place
in this world, please remember

that this world is your home.

Find home in the eyes of the beautiful stranger,
find home in the laugh of the children in the
street,
find home in the leaves rustling and the flowers
blooming,
find home in yourself, no matter how hard that
may seem.